Talking about
Grief

A Sesame Street Resource

Marie-Therese Miller

Lerner Publications ◆ Minneapolis

Dear Grown-Up,

The more comfortable you are talking with children about the challenges they face, the more of a difference you can make in their lives. In this series, *Sesame Street* friends provide caregivers and educators a starting point to discuss, process, and offer support on tough topics. Together, we can help kids learn coping and resilience-building techniques to help them face tough challenges such as divorce, grief, and more.

Sincerely,
the Editors at Sesame Workshop

Table of Contents

Talking About Death

When a person dies, their heart stops beating, and they stop breathing.

It can be hard when someone you love dies. You miss being with them.

What Is Grief?

Grief is the hurt you feel when someone you love dies. You might have lots of big feelings. You might feel sad, confused, scared, or angry.

When Elmo's Uncle Jack died, Elmo cried.

Your big feelings might last a long time. These feelings might come and go.

All of your feelings are important.

You can talk to a grown-up about how you feel.
They will take care of you and love you.

You might have lots of memories about the person who died. It helps to share these stories with other people.

It helps to share hugs too!

You can think about them any time. You can look at photos. You can draw a picture of something fun you did together, like going to the park or having story time.

Elmo remembers when Uncle Jack taught Elmo how to hit a ball.

15

You might keep some things that remind you of them, like a photo or their favorite book.

You could visit a place you used to go together.

You can do something special to remember the person you love. You can bake a cake for their birthday with the help of a grown-up.

You feel grief when someone you love dies, but you can keep memories of them in your heart.

The love you shared is always with you.

What You Can Do

You can make a memory box to remember your loved one. Decorate a box any way you want. Fill it with photos and special things that remind you of them.

Glossary

bake: to cook with heat, usually in an oven

grief: the hurt you feel when someone you love dies

memories: things you remember

picture: a drawing, painting, or photo

Read More

Gaertner, Meg. *Grief and Loss*. Mankato, MN: Little Blue House, 2022.

Leigh, Korie. *What Does Grief Feel Like?* Illustrated by Mike Malbrough. Minneapolis: Free Spirit, 2023.

Miller, Marie-Therese. *Talking about Illness: A Sesame Street ® Resource*. Minneapolis: Lerner Publications, 2025.

Explore more resources that help kids (and their grown-ups!) provided by Sesame Workshop, the nonprofit educational organization behind Sesame Street. Visit https://sesameworkshop.org/tough-topics/.

Photo Acknowledgments

Image credits: Ground Picture/Shutterstock, p. 4; supersizer/E+/Getty Images, p. 6; Westend61/Getty Images, p. 8; skynesher/E+/Getty Images, p. 9; SDI Productions/E+/Getty Images, p. 10; MoMo Productions/DigitalVision/Getty Images, pp. 12, 18 (middle); Jose Luis Pelaez Inc/DigitalVision/Getty Images, p. 14; jfairone/E+/Getty Images, p. 15; zeljkosantrac/E+/Getty Images, p. 16 (top); maroke/iStock/Getty Images, p. 16 (bottom); Hispanolistic/E+/Getty Images Plus/Getty Images, p. 17; Witthaya Prasongsin/Moment/Getty Images, p. 18 (top); Ariel Skelley/The Image Bank/Getty Images, p. 19; Kristin Zecchinelli/Moment/Getty Images, p. 21.

Cover: Catherine Falls Commercial/Moment/Getty Images.

Index

To Greyson, who loves and misses his dad, and to Michelle, who helps him grieve

Lerner Publications Company
An imprint of Lerner Publishing Group, Inc.
241 First Avenue North
Minneapolis, MN 55401 USA

For reading levels and more information, look up this title at www.lernerbooks.com.

Main body text set in Mikado. Typeface provided by HVD.

Editor: Annie Zheng **Designer:** Laura Otto Rinne

Library of Congress Cataloging-in-Publication Data

Names: Miller, Marie-Therese, author.
Title: Talking about grief : a Sesame Street resource / Marie-Therese Miller.
Description: Minneapolis, MN : Lerner Publications, [2025] | Series: Sesame Street tough topics | Includes bibliographical references and index. | Audience: Ages 4–8 | Audience: Grades K–1 | Summary: "Sometimes a person we love dies. It can hurt, and it can be scary. Sesame Street friends reassure young readers that it's OK to grieve and there are ways to remember the ones they've lost"— Provided by publisher.
Identifiers: LCCN 2023035527 (print) | LCCN 2023035528 (ebook) | ISBN 9798765620168 (library binding) | ISBN 9798765629680 (paperback) | ISBN 9798765637401 (epub)
Subjects: LCSH: Grief—Juvenile literature. | Grief in children—Juvenile literature.
Classification: LCC BF723.G75 M55 2025 (print) | LCC BF723.G75 (ebook) | DDC 155.9/37083—dc23/eng/20231218

LC record available at https://lccn.loc.gov/2023035527
LC ebook record available at https://lccn.loc.gov/2023035528

Manufactured in the United States of America
1-1009960-51821-12/18/2023